WOMEN WITH ADHD

Harnessing Your ADHD Superpowers - A woman's guide to transforming ADHD challenges into strengths at every stage of life

Dori Natasha Gentlekins

CONTENTS

INTRODUCTION

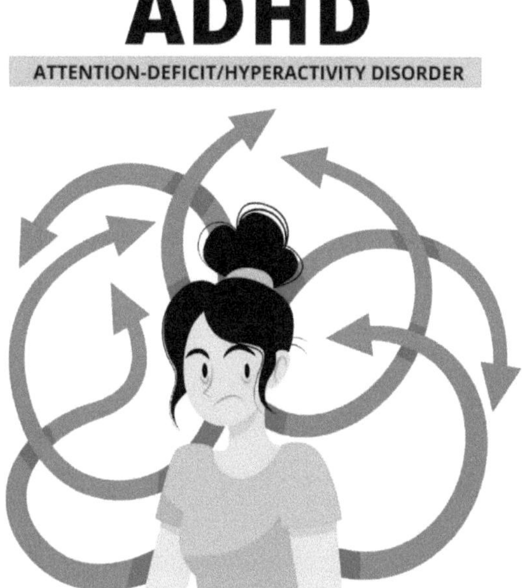

Let's be real; The effects of attention deficit hyperactivity disorder (ADHD), specifically in adult women, have received little research interest. It wouldn't be wrong to say that most of the research done on ADHD has primarily been focused on teens, kids, and men. Research involving children indicates boys receive precise ADHD diagnoses more frequently than girls. While we can point our fingers at gender bias and/or ignored ADHD symptoms, this is clearly an important issue as it has diverse effects on a woman's life if overlooked (Sreenivas, 2023).

The pathway for women looking for support and acknowledgement has become quite difficult because of the misunderstandings and preconceptions that have been reinforced by this *outrageous* lack of attention.

You can learn more about ADHD symptoms by going to this link: https://www.webmd.com/add-adhd/childhood-adhd/adhd-symptoms

Understanding the basics of ADHDin women

Let's begin with the basics. Attention deficit hyperactivity disorder, also known as ADHD, is a neurodevelopmental disorder that affects millions of individuals globally. While in many cases, it is diagnosed quite early in young hyperactive boys (imagine bouncing off walls and climbing trees like a human tornado), ADHD doesn't suddenly go away as we get older. Nope, if gone undiagnosed, it becomes a constant companion that influences our thoughts, emotions, and interactions with the outside world.

This is where it gets interesting: There is no *one-size-fits-all* treatment for ADHD. Although you'll see certain indicators or characteristics that all ADHD *sufferers* have, such as impulsivity, hyperactivity, and trouble paying attention, however each person's experience with the disorder can be very different. Furthermore, women with ADHD sometimes have unusually *cunning symptoms.*

Why and how cunning? Well, picture this: Sarah is a successful marketing manager who seems to be happy with her hectic job and social life on the *surface*. The job pays well, so what's there to complain about? However, her impulsivity and hyperactivity cause her to grapple with incomplete projects, late deliveries, and missed appointments—all symptoms of undiagnosed ADHD. She is intelligent, but her hectic personal and work life leaves her feeling overwhelmed and frustrated all the time, so much so that she has thoughts of resigning! She has always assumed her problems result from peculiarities in her personality rather than ADHD. *It's just like what we always say when things go south*: *it's just the way I am!*

Her experience dispels the myth that ADHD exclusively affects boys who are hyperactive and emphasizes the importance of raising awareness of the disorder in adult women, whose symptoms are frequently ignored or misinterpreted.

Debunking common misconceptions

Now, let us debunk a few myths, shall we? Because when we try to understand attention deficit hyperactivity disorder (ADHD) in women, misconceptions often cloud reality. So, clear the air and shed light on these misguided beliefs. From debunking the idea that ADHD is exclusive to boys to addressing the misguided belief that it signifies laziness or lack of intelligence, we'll bust these misconceptions one by one.

ADHD is not a boy thing: It's a misconception that ADHD is just a "***boy thing***." Women and girls also have ADHD, but because of our more *internalized* and *subtle* symptoms and the fact that we're not demonstrating typical symptoms that are often associated with ADHD, we usually go unnoticed.But believe me, our brains are still chugging along with ADHD in the background, even if we are not yelling it from the rooftops.

Furthermore, renowned institutions such as The American Psychiatric Association, the Centers for Disease Control and Prevention, and the National Institutes of Health all acknowledge that ADHD is an irregularity in terms of how the cerebral cortex evolves(Lange et al., 2010). According to many studies, it is caused by an imbalance of chemical transmitters, or neurotransmitters, in the cerebral cortex. Its main symptoms include impulsivity, hyperactivity, and lack of attention.

ADHD is a symptom of intelligence deficit or laziness: It's a common misconception that people with ADHD are irresponsible or lazy. In actuality, motivation or intelligence has nothing to do with ADHD. Despite having high levels of intelligence and creativity, many individuals with ADHD have trouble with organizational skills like planning and time management.

It's not that dangerous to have ADHD: Although not fatal, ADHD can have a significant negative impact on an individual's general lifestyle. Individuals with ADHD are more inclined to have anxiety, depression, and drug abuse disorders. It's also imperative to note here that ADHD patients frequently report finding it challenging to meet employment commitments and being under continual observation or supervision. So, what does this indicate? It simply means ADHD individuals have to constantly worry about losing their jobs and running out of money, which can have a negative impact on their personal lives.

The importance of diagnosis

Ah, yes, the misleading diagnosis of ADHD. Let's talk about the elephant in the room, shall we? Many women live their lives with ADHD for years, sometimes even decades, without even realizing that they suffer from a disorder that can be actually treated. We attribute our inattention, impulsiveness, and disarray to our unique personalities or simple forgetfulness.

However, accepting and acknowledging ADHD isn't about assigning a name to it; rather, it's about learning why our brain functions the way it does and how we can develop coping mechanisms for circumstances that aren't always created with ADHD in mind. To understand why ADHD in women is often delayed and the impact this delay has, we need to first understand the diagnosis rate of this disorder and why there is an imbalance in the prevalent rate. According to a study, the diagnosis rate for ADHD is about 69% more prevalent among US men than in American women, although prevalence rates by gender have become somewhat equivalent. In the United States, 4.4% of men and 3.2% of women have been diagnosed with the disorder (Polanczyk et al., 2007). Why is this so? Well, because there is a certain typical perception attached to ADHD in women. Yes, I'm talking about inattentiveness, which is sometimes overlooked in this disorder and is thought to be just a ***woman thing***. This explains why women with ADHD continue to receive little research, misdiagnose, and ignore their condition. Other elements, such as gender role expectations, socialization, and relationship dynamics, have compelled many women to mask their symptoms and issues.

How this book will help women harness their ADHD

So, you probably have a lot of questions regarding ADHD you need answered. This book will provide you with a thorough road map for steering through the complicated journey of a woman dealing with ADHD. With important insights, techniques, and support catered especially for difficulties and experiences faced by women with ADHD, this book is definitely a reliable ally. Each chapter is carefully written to provide readers with knowledge that will ultimately help them address the common misconceptions of ADHD and how a timely diagnosis can be helpful.

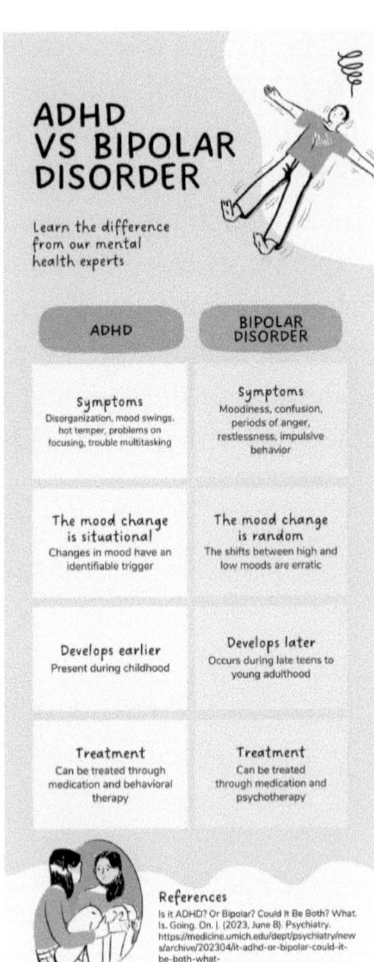
ADHD VS BIPOLAR DISORDER
Learn the difference from our mental health experts
ADHD
BIPOLAR DISORDER
Symptoms
Disorganization, mood swings, hot temper, problems on focusing, trouble multitasking
Symptoms
Moodiness, confusion, periods of anger, restlessness, impulsive behavior
The mood change is situational
Changes in mood have an identifiable trigger
The mood change is random
The shifts between high and low moods are erratic
Develops earlier
Present during childhood
Develops later
Occurs during late teens to young adulthood
Treatment
Can be treated through medication and behavioral therapy
Treatment
Can be treated through medication and psychotherapy
References
Is it ADHD? Or Bipolar? Could It Be Both? What. Is. Going. On. |. (2023, June 8). Psychiatry. https://medicine.umich.edu/dept/psychiatry/news/archive/202304/it-adhd-or-bipolar-could-it-be-both-what-going#:~:text=The%20biggest%20difference%20between%20the,Stanford%20University%20School%20of%20Medicine.

Chapter 1

Ah, the *chaotic* adolescent years – a hormonal roller-coaster of emotions and, in some cases, the extra burden of ADHD. ADHD develops initially in childhood and, in the majority of cases, continues into adulthood. For young individuals with ADHD, the shift from adolescence to adulthood is a sensitive period that may be linked to multiple medical conditions and adverse outcomes.

This chapter will examine the journey of teenage girls with ADHD, covering everything from recognizing symptoms to creating a support system and everything in between.

Identifying symptoms

As if being a teenage girl wasn't already difficult enough, add ADHD to the equation, and you have yourself a true enigma. Girls with ADHD typically have less obvious and internalized symptoms, whereas boys with the disorder frequently exhibit more overt signs like hyperactivity and impulsivity. Important yet normal symptoms such as inattention, daydreaming, and trouble maintaining an organized life – all of which can go unnoticed if you're not paying close attention (Rooney & Rooney, 2023).

Gender and ADHD

According to a study published *as Sex differences in ADHD: Conference summary* by Arnold L.E, It wouldn't be wrong to say that a usual explanation for the observed gender disparities in the diagnosis of ADHD in teenage girls is the fact that girls with ADHD are more inclined to show overwhelmingly inattentive symptoms instead of the typical disruptive hyperactive/impulsive symptoms we see in boys. Apart from this, a great number of internalizing signs like anxiety and depression also result in alternative diagnoses. As a result, teenage girls are not referred for diagnosis or treatment. This may cause more issues along the road (Le, 1996).

According to an investigative article by Rae Jacobson called *How Girls with ADHD Are Different* untreated ADHD can negatively affect teenage girls' confidence. Their mental health can be severely impacted. Contrary to this, boys who have ADHD usually take their frustrations out on others. However, girls with ADHD bottle up their hurt and rage. Due to this, they are more inclined to experience eating disorders, anxiety, and helplessness. Compared to other females, girls with untreated ADHD are also more likely to experience difficulties in their personal relationships, social interactions, and education (Jacobson et al., 2024).

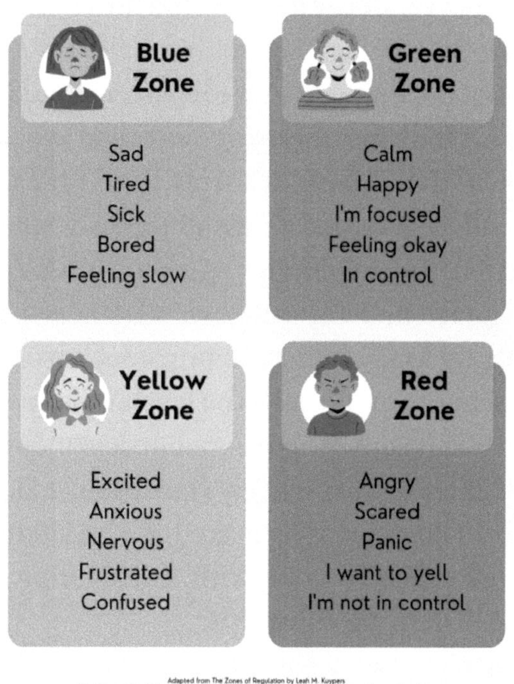

Adapted from The Zones of Regulation by Leah M. Kuypers
https://www.whitbyschool.org/passionforlearning/teaching-self-control-in-lower-elementary-with-zones-of-regulation

Navigating school challenges

What's a better way to define high school than a fuming melting pot of peer pressure, academic pressure, and frequent and unexpected pop quizzes? And for girls with ADHD, this all may seem like a never-ending cycle. The struggles to remain focused in class and failing to do so are common among people living with ADHD, and for these students, it may feel like they're swimming against the tide.

In the article *How Girls with ADHD Are Different*, author Rae Jacobson argues that today, kids have more responsibilities and possibilities than ever before. Everyone is talking about how busy they are and how over-scheduled their life is. Kids in high school have already decided on their career path. Prospects for dream college entrance are high. There is ten times more pressure than ever to achieve this dream and multitask. It's truly crazy! It's normal for a normal kid to go crazy doing all this. So, what has this done to ADHD kids? Well, girls specifically who previously used to manage and control their ADHD symptoms are now unable to do so. A girl who previously used to do fine in middle school now seems to be juggling high school academics, social dynamics, and extracurricular engagements unsuccessfully and ineffectively (Jacobson et al., 2024).

So, how could these girls make their academic life less stressful and easier to cope with, considering they have ADHD? Well, here are some tips:

Create a structured routine: Structure, structure, and structure. You need to have a daily routine that can provide you with a sense of predictability and stability. Set specific times for studying, completing assignments, and attending classes, and stick to them as much as possible.

Use visual organizers: Visual aids such as color-coded calendars, to-do lists, and graphic organizers can help ADHD girls visualize tasks and deadlines in a better way.

Break down your assignments into smaller and manageable chunks to prevent feeling overwhelmed.

Utilize technology: Embrace technology as a tool for organization and time management. Digital calendars, reminder apps, and task-tracking software can help ADHD girls manage their assignments and stick to appointments.

Practice active listening: Develop active listening skills during classes by sitting in the front row, maintaining eye contact with the teacher, and taking detailed notes. Use active listening techniques, such as summarizing key points and asking clarifying questions to enhance comprehension.

Ask for support: Don't hesitate to ask for support from teachers, school counsellors, or support groups for students with ADHD. Surround yourself with understanding peers and mentors who can offer encouragement and assistance whenever you need it.

Addressing and overcoming self-esteem issues

In their article *You Are Not the Sum of Your ADHD Challenges,* Michelle Frank, Psy.D. and Sari Solden, M.S. , LMFT argue that perceiving the world in black-or-white, all-or-nothing is how the ADHD brain works. The issue lies in the complexity and inconsistencies in human nature. Because of this, many women with ADHD swing between extreme self-perceptions, such as being excellent or horrible, intelligent or stupid, ambitious or sluggish. Inner reflection and a good dosage of self-acceptance should take the place of this reactive, harsh thinking, which lowers one's self-esteem (PsyD, 2021).

Here's how you can address this issue:

1. ***Shift your perspective from fixing yourself to embracing yourself:*** A positive first step is acknowledging that our body and minds are not entirely distinct entities. Let go of the belief that you need fixing; you are already whole, worthy, and deserving of love.

2. ***Take a "Yes, and... " stance:*** Create empowering affirmations like, "I *acknowledge my challenges and celebrate my progress, no matter how small, and improve my self-care*," or "*I can accomplish these things even though I still struggle.*" We need to constantly remind ourselves that having abilities and flaws in the same body is perfectly normal and acceptable and helps us manage our issues with self-compassion, which is essential for bringing about lasting and real change.

3. ***Exploring your ADHD advantages and opportunities for improvement:*** You are well aware of the difficulties that ADHD presents. You might have even given them quite a lot of attention. But considering your challenges and your strengths can help you see the entire picture. The whole you. However, a lot of individuals have trouble seeing these areas or how to tap into them. In the next

section, we have listed some ADHD questions you can ask yourself to challenge these ideas.

Practical tools and techniques for managing symptoms

As discussed in the last sections, it's about time you start asking your ADHD some serious questions. Chances are, you will see a bigger picture of more than what your ADHD lets you see.

Assessing your strengths

1. What are you really good at that feels easy for you?
2. What could you teach others or contribute to their lives?
3. What skills or talents have you developed over time?

Assessing your challenges

1. What ADHD symptoms do you find most difficult?
2. Can you describe the daily struggles or obstacles you face because of these challenges?
3. How does ADHD affect your life, even if you're

getting treatment?

Trust Your Inner Guidance

Although we discuss the significance of following or having principles, we hardly ever follow them, right? It's important for teenage girls who experience the constant tug of ADHD to reflect and find within themselves an inner guide or personal direction that will help them determine what kind of life they want to lead.

When you're stuck in a loop, pause and reconnect with your core principles and inner self. Amidst confusion or intense emotions, trusting your inner guidance and staying true to your beliefs leads to wiser choices instead of being swayed by ADHD distractions.

Knowing your inner values will help you create a statement of purpose for yourself.

Create your own statement of purpose in order to create your own unique inner guidance, and start living life the way you want to, which aligns with your values and strengths; take a moment to read these questions and provide honest answers:

What is the most important thing to you?

Which values do you stand for?

What do you want to be an example of in life?

What fundamental beliefs guide you?

What message do you want to get across to people?

What kind of legacy do you hope to leave behind when you look back on your life?

Support Systems

A research study called *Do different factors influence whether girls versus boys meet ADHD diagnostic criteria? Sex differences among children with high ADHD symptoms* has contributed immensely to understanding the role of the family in supporting ADHD teens. The study looks at how ADHD symptoms can affect how well students do in school. What they found was that having more ADHD symptoms could lead to issues at home and less support from friends and teachers, which could make it harder for students to do well in school. The researchers studied over 2,000 students in the Netherlands from when they were around 11 years old until they were 19. The study found that ADHD symptoms were linked to problems at home, less support from teachers and friends, and lower levels of education as they got older (Mowlem et al., 2019).

Parenting a teenager with ADHD can be tough. You need extra patience with such teens as they become more independent. Yet, they still need guidance and support from their parents. So, here's what you as a parent can do:

Learn about ADHD: Educate yourself about ADHD to understand your teen's behaviors better. Knowing more about ADHD can help you feel more patient and less frustrated.

Talk about ADHD and goals: Have open conversations with your teen about how ADHD affects them in different areas of their life. Show empathy and understanding.

Normalize ADHD: Remind your teen that having ADHD is not a fault, but it's important to discuss areas where they can improve.

Provide hands-on help: Assist your teen with tasks that may be challenging due to ADHD, such as organizing their room. Work on these tasks together patiently and make it fun if possible.

Teach social skills: Help your teen develop social skills by addressing behaviors that may affect their friendships, such as interrupting or not listening well. Offer specific strategies for improvement.

Continue treatment: Ensure your teen continues with their ADHD treatment, which may include medication, therapy, and school support. Regularly assess their needs and goals with the help of professionals.

Maintain a positive relationship: Avoid excessive criticism and focus on maintaining a positive relationship with your teen. Criticism can lead to feelings of insecurity and may worsen behavior. Instead, provide support and encouragement.

Making school more supportive

Teachers, too, can play a positive role when lending a hand to ADHD teenage girls. To begin with, teachers *should* adjust the school environment to better suit students with ADHD. Here are some changes that might help your student succeed academically:

1. Provide options for assignments, such as written essays, online quizzes, or hands-on projects.

2. Allow extra time for tasks and tests and give them breaks during tests.

3. Break learning tasks into smaller, more manageable chunks.

The important thing to take from this section is that we all should sit together and devise an effective learning strategy and an individualized learning plan for every child with ADHD. We can support our teenagers if we all work together as a team, playing our roles in a very positive way conducive to a positive environment.

CHAPTER 2

As you enter the workforce, you'll enter a new phase of your life. A phase that is full of opportunities and challenges. In this chapter, we'll see how teenagers with ADHD can manage their jobs effectively. We'll talk about picking the right career and doing great work once you're there. We'll share tips and advice to help you use your strengths to succeed at work. With these practical tips, you'll have what you need to do your best and thrive in your career.

Choosing a career

Choosing a career that suits your ADHD traits is like finding the perfect puzzle piece for your life. It's all about understanding what makes you tick and what you're good at. Maybe you thrive in fast-paced environments or love jobs where you can be creative. In this section, we'll talk about choosing a career that suits your ADHD traits and how to match them with your ADHD strengths. Whether you're drawn to jobs that require quick thinking or ones that let you work independently, we'll help you navigate the world of jobs and the workforce.

Self-assessment: Start by identifying your strengths, interests, and ADHD-related traits. Reflect on activities or tasks that you excel in and enjoy, as well as those that you find challenging.

Research career options: Explore various career paths and industries that align with your strengths and interests.

Consider factors such as job flexibility, stimulation, and potential for growth.

Consider the work environment: Think about the type of work environment that suits your ADHD traits. Do you thrive in fast-paced settings or prefer a more structured routine? Consider how different work environments may impact your productivity and job satisfaction.

Evaluate job requirements: Evaluate the specific requirements and responsibilities of different roles within your chosen career path. Determine if your ADHD traits align with the demands of the job and if you have the necessary skills to excel.

Seek advice and guidance: Consult with career counsellors, mentors, or professionals in your desired field for insights and advice. They can provide valuable perspectives and help you make informed decisions about your career path.

Trial and error: Don't be afraid to try out different roles or internships to gain hands-on experience and determine what works best for you. Experimenting with different career paths can help you refine your interests and preferences.

Set realistic goals: Set achievable short-term and long-term goals based on your career aspirations and ADHD traits. Break down larger goals into smaller, manageable steps to maintain focus and momentum.

Adaptability and flexibility: Stay open to adapting your career path as your interests and circumstances evolve. Flexibility is key in navigating the difficulties of career exploration and growth.

Embrace your strengths: Recognize and embrace the unique strengths and talents that come with ADHD, such as creativity, problem-solving skills, and adaptability. Leverage these strengths to your advantage in pursuing a fulfilling career.

Disclosing ADHD in professional settings

Disclosing that you have ADHD could affect your employer's opinion. However, without disclosure, there would be no safety measures and, hence, no real changes would occur. The primary thing to note here is that, as an employee or a job applicant, you are not required to disclose a medical diagnosis to the employer. In some cases or organizations, it might be a requirement to describe specific personality traits, in addition to mentioning that you have ADHD. This will help the organization deduce if you have the traits that will help you do the job. People with ADHD and other such conditions are welcomed within the HR culture of an increasing number of organizations. However, in some situations, it's best to mention that you have ADHD. Although this has clear benefits, there may occasionally be drawbacks as well.

Potential disadvantages include the possibility that you won't get hired or that it may be used as a justification for firing you, even though it is illegal in most nations to discriminate against someone based on their disability (UN disability treaty,2006). However, an organization may choose not to disclose this reason for firing or not hiring. It might also impact how your job performance is evaluated. You can face unfavorable treatment at work from your manager or coworkers if you disclose your ADHD openly. Alternatively, coworkers may occasionally overdo their helpfulness to the point where it makes you feel like someone who needs help because of this disorder.

Being comfortable with your ADHD is very important. Communicating your diagnosis can be beneficial if you've already overcome your self-esteem and are aware of your abilities and shortcomings. If you can tell the company that the "Ideal alignment of a person and a position" benefits both parties, you can actually get some really good perks, such as workable changes that can improve your performance, and you may even get permission to work a portion of the week from home. Thus, highlighting the relevant aspects of your ADHD can help you find a job that best suits your skills. There would have been no changes and no special rights if you hadn't disclosed your ADHD diagnosis. It all starts with you accepting your ADHD and aligning it to see how it can benefit for your career.

Advocacy and Legal Rights

The Americans with Disabilities Act(2008) guarantees you the right to accommodations for ADHD at work and protection from discrimination. In this section, discover the legal safeguards for adults with ADHD and what the ADA disability list has to say about ADHD.

What is the Americans with Disabilities Act?

The federal Americans with Disabilities Act, or ADA, provides the most significant legal protection for employees with ADHD. Congress passed the ADA's original version in 1990, and it was revised in 2008 to make it more broadly applicable.

Does the ADA cover ADHD?

There is no doubt that the ADA provides coverage for people with ADHD, regardless of whether you see ADHD as neurological, impacting how the brain concentrates or thinks, or as a disability that interferes with functioning.

What is meant by "fair accommodations"?

When an employer receives applications from qualified individuals with disabilities, they are required to provide reasonable adjustments for them. For instance, if an employee discloses their ADHD to their employer, provides medical records, or discusses how ADHD affects them at work with HR or management, they may request accommodations. However, it's important to understand that the employer isn't obligated to make changes that are unreasonable, costly, or disruptive to the business. Some common "reasonable" accommodations for ADHD include:

1. Creating a calm work environment
2. Allowing the use of white noise machines or noise-cancelling headphones

3. Offering the option to work remotely, part-time or full-time

4. Taking breaks as needed

5. Streamlining tasks to focus on essential responsibilities

6. Permitting the use of assistive technology like calendars, apps, or timers

7. Adjusting tests, curriculum, or guidelines

8. Considering reassignment to an open position

Understanding Your Rights

Before seeking legal advice from an advocate or representative, we suggest checking out the directory of legal resources below. These resources can help you find the right support or legal representation (Yellin, 2023).

Also, don't forget to visit ADDA's ADHD @ Work website! The entire website is dedicated to providing you with the best information on ADHD in the workplace. If you're struggling to get accommodations at work, start by visiting.

- ***The Injury Claim Coach*** website offers a unique feature – a live Q&A function where users can interact with a former judge for expert advice on specific issues. Additionally, they provide access to an Equal Employment Opportunity Guideline.

https://www.injuryclaimcoach.com/

- ***The Council of Parents Attorneys and Advocates (COPAA)*** is dedicated to safeguarding the civil and legal rights of students with disabilities. With a network of attorneys, they can assist with challenges related to high-stakes exams and accommodations for postsecondary education.
- Since 1977, ***the Association for Higher Education and Disabilities (AHEAD)*** has been a valuable resource for ensuring students with disabilities receive necessary accommodations from early childhood education to post-secondary education.

Professional Growth: Long-term career planning

Steering through the complex professional landscape can be quite challenging, especially for women with ADHD (Acc, 2022). However, with careful planning and strategic approaches, it's possible to achieve long-term career growth and success. Here are some key strategies you can consider:

Identify strengths and interests: Start by identifying your strengths, interests, and values. Understanding what motivates you and where your strengths lie can help you align your career goals accordingly.

Set clear career goals: Define your long-term career goals and break them down into smaller, actionable chunks. Setting clear objectives will provide you with a roadmap and help you stay focused on your professional journey.

Seek continuous learning opportunities: Invest in your professional development by looking out for learning opportunities, such as workshops, courses, and certifications. Continuous learning not only enhances your skills, but also shows your commitment to personal growth.

Build a supportive network: Surround yourself with supportive mentors, peers, and professional individuals. Networking can provide valuable insights, opportunities, and support throughout your career journey.

Advocate for yourself: Don't be afraid to advocate for yourself and your career aspirations. Speak up about your achievements, goals, and the support you need to succeed. Confidence and self-advocacy are essential skills for career advancement.

Embrace flexibility: Recognize that career paths are rarely linear and may require flexibility and adaptability. Be open to exploring new opportunities, taking on challenges, and adjusting your goals as needed.

By incorporating these strategies into your career planning and development, you can position yourself for long-term professional growth and fulfillment despite the challenges of ADHD.

CHAPTER 3

For women with ADHD, steering through relationships and social interactions can be quite complicated. In this chapter, we will see how ADHD affects interpersonal interactions, including friendships, romantic partnerships, and family dynamics. Whether you're looking for advice on dating, keeping friends, or healing family relationships, this chapter provides insightful guidance on the challenges of interpersonal interactions.

Communication Skills

ADHD can affect your personal relationships, causing misunderstandings, disappointments, and frustration. The symptoms of ADHD, such as distractibility, disorganization, and impulsivity, can create challenges in your closest relationships, especially if the condition hasn't been diagnosed or treated.

You may feel you're constantly criticized or micromanaged by your partner, leading to feelings of dissatisfaction and frustration in the relationship. However, it's possible to improve your partnership and cultivate a happier, healthier relationship despite the challenges of ADHD (Hassall and Barrett, 2022).

Here are a few easy strategies to increase mutual understanding in your relationship: **Learn as much as you can about ADHD:** Gaining knowledge about ADHD and its signs or symptoms is a step towards a mutual understanding of the impact this disorder may have on your relationship. Acknowledging that individuals with ADHD function differently can ease witnessing the symptoms for the non-ADHD partner and bring relief to the ADHD p artner.**Recognize the effects of symptoms of ADHD**: It's critical to recognize the negative effects of untreated ADHD symptoms on a relationship when one partner has the disorder. The non-ADHD partner should also think about how their behavior, such as nagging or criticizing, may affect the ADHD-er and the overall relationship. It's critical that we gently address each other's concerns rather than brushing them off. **Distinguish the individual from the symptoms**: Acknowledge your partner's carelessness or hyperactivity as signs of ADHD rather than assigning them "a label". Recall that these symptoms are not personal qualities.

In order to resolve issues in a relationship, communication is essential. If emotions are running high during a discussion, take breaks and pay close attention to each other. Instead of being sucked into the debate, attempt to understand the fundamental problem (Wymbs et al., 2021).Managing Emotional Responses

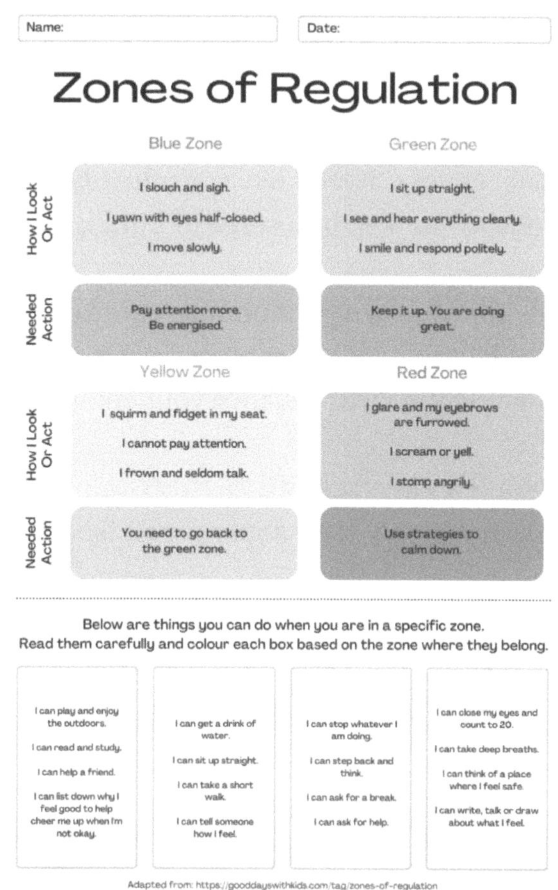

For individuals with ADHD, social interactions can be quite overwhelming due to impulsivity and intensified emotions. In this section, we explore strategies to help manage these emotional responses effectively. From recognizing triggers to developing coping mechanisms, we

will provide practical advice for keeping composure and fostering positive social connections.

Managing intense emotions and less well-known symptoms, such as emotional regulation issues, can be difficult for many people with ADHD (Sosnoski, 2021). You may be doing just fine, and then suddenly something triggers you, and suddenly, you're overcome with strong emotions that you just can't control. It feels like your already overworked brain is being overtaken by a surge of hurt, irritation, fear, or anxiety.

Methods for improving emotional controlFortunately, there are achievable and effective strategies you can put into practice right now to enhance your emotional regulation.

Here are a few easy tactics:

- Take a moment to recognize your feelings.
- Establish a strategy to assist you in regaining your composure and pausing.
- Think about taking a quick break to clean your face, get some fresh air, or listen to relaxing music.
- Take part in mindfulness exercises, including mindful yoga, body scans, and sitting meditation. By bringing consciousness to the present, mindfulness can help refocus intense emotions and fosters the development of emotional awareness.
- Be aware of negative thought patterns, such as rumination, catastrophizing, blaming others, or

self-blame.

- Try changing the way you think about things by focusing on the good or letting go of the things you can't control.
- Emotional control and mental efficiency can both be enhanced by regular cardiovascular activity.
- Exercises that aren't cardio based may still be beneficial for ADHD symptoms.

When to get assistance

Seeking support from a healthcare professional is a good idea if you're having a lot of trouble controlling your emotions or experiencing extreme social anxiety. They can offer direction, suggest therapy, or put you in touch with support groups so you can successfully manage the emotional regulation issues that come with ADHD.

CHAPTER 4

Being a mother is an amazing and life-changing experience that comes with endless joy, challenges, and, well ... chores. The shift to motherhood can be especially difficult for women with ADHD, since they have to balance the demands of raising children with their disorder. This chapter delves into the experiences and difficulties faced by moms who have ADHD, covering everything from parenting techniques to getting professional support. To mothers with ADHD, we provide insights, support, and useful advice on maintaining daily routines and building relationships with their kids.

Pregnancy planning and management

Organizing an ADHD Pregnancy Make sure you are using a reliable method of birth control until you speak with your physician. Plan your pregnancy to minimize risks to you and your unborn child by giving yourself enough time to make changes to your mental health medication under your physician's supervision. It is important to speak with your doctor about the safety of taking ADHD medication while pregnant, as stopping the drug abruptly could worsen the symptoms (Other Disorders and Pregnancy, n.d.). In case medicine is required during pregnancy, your physician might recommend amphetamines or methylphenidate because they have well-established safety records. If you find out you are pregnant, let your midwife or healthcare team know right away. Before changing your medication, talk to them about your options.

Strategies for managing daily routines and parenting

Raising children, running your household, and looking after your mental wellness are huge challenges for any parent with ADHD. Since ADHD affects almost every aspect of parenting, parents who have the disorder require resources and help to properly manage their symptoms and look after their children's requirements at every developmental stage (Josel, 2021).

Here are some strategies for parents with ADHD to manage daily routines and parenting duties effectively:

Establish consistent routines: Create consistent schedules for meals, bedtime, and other daily activities. Consistency can help both parents and children know what to expect and reduce stress.

Use visual reminders: Utilize visual aids, such as calendars, to-do lists, and task charts to keep track of tasks and deadlines. Visual reminders can be helpful for parents with ADHD to stay organized.

Break tasks into smaller steps: Break down larger tasks into smaller, more manageable steps. This approach can prevent you from feeling overwhelmed and make tasks feel more achievable.

Set up organizational systems: Implement organizational systems such as labelled storage bins, colour-coded calendars, and designated spaces for important items to minimize clutter and streamline daily routines.

Prioritize self-care: Prioritize self-care activities such as adequate sleep, healthy eating, regular exercise, and relaxation techniques. Taking care of your own well-being is essential for managing ADHD symptoms and being present for your children.

Delegate responsibilities: Delegate tasks to other family members whenever possible. Sharing responsibilities can lighten the load and prevent burnout.

Use technology wisely: Take advantage of technology tools such as reminder apps, alarm clocks, and digital calendars to stay organized and on track with daily routines.

Be kind to yourself: Finally, remember to be compassionate toward yourself. Parenting with ADHD presents unique challenges, and it's okay to acknowledge when things don't go as planned. Celebrate your successes and practice self-compassion along the way.

The genetics of ADHD

After decades of research (Faraone & Larsson, 2018), it has been found that genes are a major factor in the development of ADHD and how it connects to other disorders. Research on twins, adoptive children, and families has shown that ADHD often runs in families. Researchers are looking for certain genes connected to ADHD since they have found that *genetics* account for approximately 74% of the disorder's causes. Numerous genomic locations have been linked to ADHD by research employing genome-wide association studies (GWAS) and genetic linkage. These studies have also shown that numerous common genetic variants, each with a tiny effect, account for a considerable percentage of the hereditary influence of ADHD.

Self-Care Strategies: Importance of self-care for mothers with ADHD

Self-care for mothers is crucial but also challenging to prioritize, particularly with ADHD. However, self-care can begin simply, such as monitoring your mood, practicing relaxation, and gradually expanding it to incorporate time-management practices. Start now with these eight suggestions for ADHD mothers' self-care.

Embrace imperfection: Let go of the pressure to be the perfect parent. It's okay to make mistakes and learn from them. Give yourself permission to be imperfect and embrace the beautiful messiness of motherhood.

Practice mindfulness: Set aside a few minutes each day to practice mindfulness or meditation. Focus on your breath, tune into your body, and let go of racing thoughts. Mindfulness can help calm the mind and reduce stress.

Set realistic expectations: Be realistic about what you can accomplish in a day. Break tasks into smaller, manageable steps and celebrate small victories. Remember, it's okay to ask for help when needed.

Prioritize Sleep: As we've mentioned before, make sleep a priority. Create a calming bedtime routine, limit screen time before bed, and create a comfortable sleep environment.

Nurture connections: Cultivate meaningful connections with friends, family, and support groups. Share your experiences, seek advice, and lean on your support network when needed.

Move your body: Incorporate regular physical activity into your routine. Whether it's a brisk walk, yoga session, or dance party with your kids, find activities that energize and uplift you.

Support networks for mothers

As mothers, we often find ourselves wearing multiple hats and juggling countless responsibilities. While the journey of motherhood is incredibly rewarding, it can also be overwhelming. That's why it's essential to remember that you don't have to go through it alone. Building a support network of fellow moms, community resources, and professional support systems can make all the difference in your experience as a mother (Anderson, 2022).

How to leverage support networks:

Connect with fellow moms: Reach out to other moms in your community or online who share similar experiences and challenges. Join mom groups, parenting classes, or support groups where you can connect with other mothers, share advice, and offer each other encouragement and support. Remember, there is strength in solidarity, and you'll find comfort in knowing that you're not alone on this journey.

Seek professional guidance: Don't hesitate to seek professional guidance if you're struggling with mental health issues, relationship challenges, or other stressors. Therapists, counsellors, and mental health professionals can provide you with valuable support, guidance, and coping mechanisms.

Explore community resources: Take advantage of community resources and support services available to mothers in your area. From parenting workshops and childcare assistance to breastfeeding support groups and postpartum mental health services, there is often a variety of resources available to help you steer through the challenges of motherhood.

Make self-care a priority: Remember to prioritize self-care and make time for activities that nourish your mind, body, and soul. Whether it's taking a walk in nature, practicing yoga, or indulging in a hobby you love, self-care is essential for maintaining your well-being as a mother.

Be open to receiving help: "*It takes a village to raise a child*", so there's no shame in seeking support when you need it. Whether it's asking a friend to watch your kids for a few hours, accepting a meal delivery from a neighbor, or reaching out to a family member for emotional support, allow yourself to receive help with gratitude and appreciation.

CHAPTER 5

In this chapter, we will delve into a phase that is often overlooked but is equally significant: ADHD after menopause, also known as the golden years.

Menopause marks the end of a woman's reproductive years, bringing with it hormonal changes and shifts in both physical and emotional well-being. While attention is given to the symptoms and experiences of menopause itself, the impact of added diagnoses, such as ADHD, during this stage of life is not always fully understood or addressed.

Changing Symptoms

The Impact of Menopause on ADHD Your periods become less regular and your body's estrogen levels stay lower for prolonged periods of time during the perimenopause, which is the phase preceding menopause. Perimenopause typically lasts five to eight years, though this varies from person to person. If you haven't had a period in a year, you are said to be in menopause. In the United States, the average age of menopause is 51. Many women experience symptoms such as depression, difficulty focusing, memory and sleep issues, in addition to the physical changes that occur before, during, and after menopause. This makes it more difficult for those who have ADHD to focus and plan ahead.

The added complexities of life, hormonal fluctuations, and ADHD can provide a challenging scenario for women who are in their late 40s and beyond. Hormonal changes during this time may cause you to feel more *overwhelmed* than normal if you have mild ADHD. It's possible that some people are unaware they have ADHD until their symptoms get so severe that they require medical attention. Even if you've been doing a good job controlling your ADHD, it could feel more difficult at first. Furthermore, this time of life frequently comes with extra stressors. You may be looking after your children and caring for ageing parents simultaneously. As your children move out, you could be getting used to having an empty nest. You may be under a lot of pressure at work or be adjusting to big life crises like divorce or losing a spouse.

Health Management Post-menopause

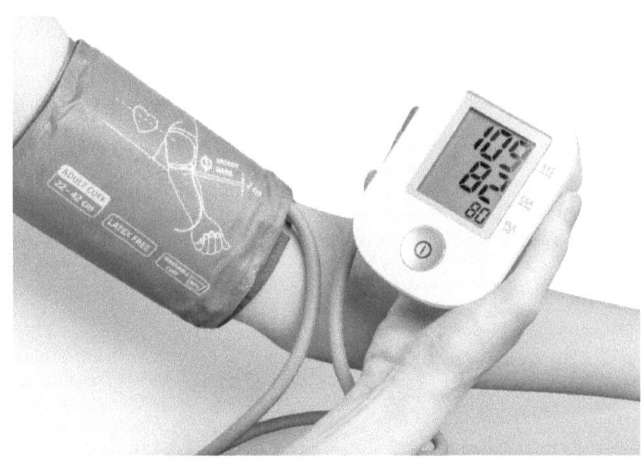
ADULT CUFF
22 - 42 cm
LATEX FREE
109
83
80

While managing ADHD in midlife might be difficult, there are strategies for gaining control over this stressor. Using a *journal* or *an app* to record your symptoms is a useful strategy. If you are still getting your period, you can consider menstrual cycle-related trends.

Consult with your physician. They may adjust the medicine or dosage if you are currently on ADHD medication. To treat your symptoms, they may also recommend additional medications like *hormone treatment* or *antidepressants*. In numerous respects, stimulants may be the answer. Studies have indicated that ***lisdexamfetamine***, also known as ***Vyvanse***, is an ADHD medication that may help premenopausal and menopausal women who are experiencing ADHD with issues like memory, task management, and organization.

Lifestyle Adjustments

Known as "hyperkinetic disorder", fifty years ago, the only symptoms of ADHD were *restlessness* and *poor impulse management*. Since then, and especially in the past ten years, our knowledge of the disorder has grown significantly. We now know that symptoms can include anything from feelings of *vulnerability* to *hyperactivity* to *lack of attention*. You can't change your genes or roll back to being ignorant that you never had ADHD, but you can consciously make lifestyle changes that will help you cope with ADHD through the years. And that's why

sleep is extremely crucial for the health of your body and brain. Although the benefits of sleep are widely acknowledged, many people – including those with ADHD – ignore them or find it difficult to fall asleep. *Engaging in physical activity* benefits not only your body but also your mind. According to research, regular exercise may help *lessen* the damaging effects of stress and trauma on the brain. Additionally, it promotes brain growth, increases cognitive function, and enhances learning, particularly in areas where attention and memory are linked to ADHD.

Your brain health is significantly affected by your diet as well. Nuts and seafood are high in omega-3 fatty acids, which are vital for brain health and can enhance neural communication. Micronutrients that are crucial for focus, attention, and impulse control include zinc, iron, and vitamin D. Your cognitive activities might not work as well if you're lacking in certain nutrients. Nutrition, exercise, and sleep are interconnected and have an impact on one another throughout your life. Consuming wholesome food provides you the energy to work out, and working out improves your quality of sleep. Strive to strike a balance between these three elements and concentrate on what suits you the most to get the greatest outcomes.

Legacy and Wisdom

Passing on the legacy of wisdom is a beautiful way to empower younger women on their journey with ADHD. By sharing the lessons learned from a lifetime of experiences and the coping strategies developed along the way, older women can offer valuable guidance and support to the next generation. This mentorship not only provides practical advice, but also instils a sense of hope and inspiration. Through open dialogue and compassionate understanding, senior women can help younger women steer through the challenges of ADHD with confidence and resilience, ensuring a brighter and more fulfilling future for all.

Here are some strategies that can help younger women cope with their ADHD. Throughout the book, we have laid great emphasis on these strategies and have discussed them thoroughly as well.

- Develop a daily routine and stick to it as much as possible.
- Break tasks into smaller, manageable steps to avoid feeling overwhelmed.
- Use visual aids such as calendars, to-do lists, and color-coding to stay organized.
- Practice mindfulness and relaxation techniques to manage stress and anxiety.
- Seek out support groups or online communities for encouragement and advice.
- Prioritize self-care activities such as exercise, healthy eating, and sufficient sleep.
- Advocate for yourself in academic and professional settings by requesting accommodations, if needed.
- Embrace your strengths and celebrate your successes, no matter how small they may seem.

- Remember to be patient and kind to yourself, acknowledging that progress takes time and effort.

Planning for Retirement

It's true that ADHD can influence your retirement planning. With ADHD, you might not manage things easily, like tracking your spending, saving money, or even considering long-term financial goals. However, the first step in making wise retirement plans is realizing these difficulties (Cfp, 2023).

Never forget that ADHD does not have to dictate your financial destiny. It just nudges you to take a slightly different approach to things. That's where having expert assistance is helpful.

Putting Retirement Plans in place with ADHD **Remain Simple** People living with ADHD may find complex financial plans burdensome. So stick with simple retirement options such as index funds, 401(k)s, and IRAs. Whenever possible, set up automatic contributions to maintain consistency (Cfp, 2023). **Set Goals That You Can See** To help you visualize your retirement goals, use vision boards, graphs, and charts. This will serve as a visual guide to help you stay motivated and focused. **Establish Achievable Goals** Divide your retirement savings targets or goals into more manageable, achievable parts. Celebrate your accomplishments and maintain an optimistic attitude.

Ensure Investment Diversification Investing in diversified portfolios helps you feel more secure and spreads out your risks. Individuals with ADHD can try a varied portfolio, which will keep them interested. If you're someone who is closer to retirement, then you should concentrate on safer solutions, while younger people can take greater risks for higher growth.

Building Retirement Savings Motivation **Frequent Check-ins**Arrange frequent check-ins and plan adjustments with your financial advisor. These check-ins help you stay responsible and enable you to adjust if your circumstances change, which they certainly will. **Conscientious Reminders** Use technology to provide periodic notifications for financial obligations and payment deadlines. You can keep on track with the help of wearable technology, calendar alerts, and smartphone apps. In order to increase your chances of success, you can even automate your investments and savings. **Make Savings More Fun** Make saving more like a game by setting goals for yourself to achieve. This can bring about an excitement to the *competitive spirit linked to ADHD*, adding interest to the procedure.

CHAPTER 6

Medication and Therapies

Overview of pharmacological treatments and psychotherapies

A particular type of remedy for emotional problems and mental health issues is *psychotherapy*. In this type of therapy, an individual or a qualified professional engages with you in full for several sessions. The type of therapy used and the treatment's aim determine how the sessions are structured. In order to address the symptoms of ADHD, doctors will often prescribe drugs, such as stimulants. Psychotherapy and medicine together can sometimes be more beneficial than either of them used alone. A review published in 2020 had 53 trails done on ADHD in adults. It discovered ample proof that psychotherapy, particularly cognitive behavioral therapy (CBT), helped lessen symptoms of ADHD (Fullen et al., 2020). Data on children with ADHD from ten types of research were included in another 2020 evaluation (Coghill et al., 2021). It was believed that children with the disorder might become less irritable and aggressive with psychotherapy. Still, it brought to light a number of shortcomings in the research, including the therapy's brief duration.

Alternative Therapies

The role of diet, exercise, and holistic treatments

Treatment and medication are effective strategies to control the symptoms of ADHD. However, they are not your *only* choices. According to recent research, practicing mindfulness meditation, which involves actively observing your thoughts and feelings as they arise, can help you focus better and relax. According to a 2017 ADDitude magazine poll, over 33% of persons with ADHD employ this strategy, and around 40% rate it highly effective. Unlike other therapies, mindfulness meditation doesn't require a visit to the therapist or a prescription. It can be done while sitting, strolling, or even doing some form of yoga.

According to research, practicing mindfulness meditation can significantly reduce the symptoms of ADHD. According to a ground-breaking study conducted by UCLA, individuals with ADHD who participated in a weekly 2-and-a-half-hour mindfulness meditation workshop and then consistently practiced at home for five to fifteen minutes each day for eight weeks showed improved task-focused attention. They had low levels of anxiety and depression as well.

Technology AidsIn recent years, there has been an increase in the development of apps designed to support individuals with ADHD. These apps offer a range of tools and resources to help manage symptoms and lead fulfilling lives. Below, we'll explore a comparison of some apps recommended by Google for people with ADHD, along with others that we've personally found beneficial.

1. **Todoist**: This app helps you stay organized by creating to-do lists, setting reminders, and scheduling tasks. It's great for keeping track of daily activities and staying on top of deadlines.

2. **Forest**: If you struggle with distractions, Forest can help. It encourages focus and productivity by al-

lowing you to plant virtual trees when you start a task. The longer you stay focused, the more your tree grows.

3. **Mindfulness Apps (e.g., Headspace, Calm):** Mindfulness can be beneficial for managing stress and improving focus. These apps offer guided meditation sessions and relaxation techniques to help you stay calm and centered throughout the day.

4. **Evernote**: Evernote is a versatile note-taking app that allows you to capture ideas, make lists, and organize your thoughts. It's useful for keeping track of important information and staying organized.

5. **Time Timer**: This visual timer app helps you manage your time more effectively by providing a clear visual representation of how much time is remaining for a task or activity. It's great for staying on track and avoiding procrastination.

6. **Pomodoro Technique Apps (e.g., Focus Booster, Tomato Timer):** The Pomodoro Technique involves working in short bursts of focused activity followed by short breaks. These apps help you implement this technique by timing your work sessions and breaks.

1. **Meal Planning Apps (e.g., Mealime, Paprika)**: Planning meals in advance can help you save time and reduce stress. These apps offer meal-planning tools, recipes, and grocery lists to simplify the process.

2. **Medication Reminder Apps (e.g., Medisafe, MyTherapy):** If you take medication for ADHD, these apps can help you stay on track with your medication schedule by sending reminders and tracking your doses.

3. **Habit Tracking Apps (e.g., Habitica, HabitBull)**: Developing and maintaining healthy habits is important for managing ADHD symptoms. These apps allow you to track your progress and stay motivated as you work towards your goals.

4. **Focus@Will**: This app provides curated music playlists designed to enhance focus and productivity. It's especially helpful for creating a distraction-free environment when you need to concentrate.

Continuous Learning and Personal Development

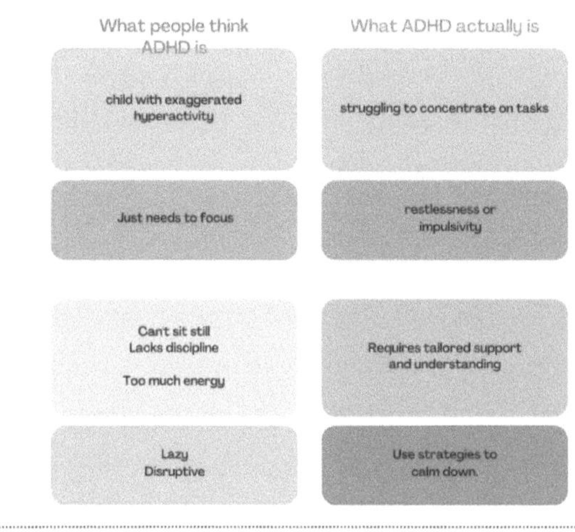

Growing knowledge of ADHD contributes to the development of inclusive, accessible healthcare, businesses, and educational institutions. Additionally, it lessens the severity of the disorder, making physicians appropriately treat ADHD and might even persuade those who exhibit symptoms to get diagnosed.

Raising Awareness

Organizations, such as Children and Adults with ADD (CHADD) host educational seminars, awareness campaigns, and events to raise awareness of ADHD and its effects throughout ADHD Awareness Month. Hospitals and mental health facilities, among other medical establishments, support awareness campaigns by using flyers, pamphlets, instructional programs, and ADHD-specific events. The website for ADHD Awareness Month offers an abundance of information, a place for people to share personal stories and tools for those who think they may have ADHD. The website also debunks myths that are widely held, such as the idea that ADHD is over diagnosed or that children are overprescribed to medicine, and clarifies that ADHD is not a choice but a behavioral problem.

Community and Advocacy

Join support groups: Participate in local or online support groups for individuals with ADHD to connect with others who understand your experiences and challenges.

Attend events: Attend ADHD awareness events, seminars, workshops, and conferences to learn more about the condition and advocate for broader awareness and support.

Share your story: Share your personal experiences with ADHD to raise awareness and help others understand the realities of living with the condition.

Volunteer: Get involved with organizations dedicated to ADHD advocacy and support by volunteering your time or skills to contribute to their initiatives and campaigns.

Educate others: Educate friends, family members, colleagues, and educators about ADHD to dispel myths and misconceptions and promote understanding and empathy.

Advocate for policy change: Advocate for policy changes at local, state, and national levels to improve access to resources, support services, and accommodations for individuals with ADHD.

Utilise social media: Use social media platforms to share informative articles, resources, and personal stories about ADHD to reach a wider audience and foster community engagement and support.

Collaborate with professionals: Collaborate with healthcare professionals, educators, employers, and policymakers to promote ADHD awareness and create supportive environments for individuals with ADHD in various settings.

CONCLUSION

We combine the key insights from each chapter, providing actionable takeaways for readers to implement in their daily lives. We emphasize empowerment and acceptance, encouraging readers to embrace their unique strengths and view ADHD as a part of their identity that can be empowering. Finally, we issue a call to action, urging ongoing engagement with the ADHD community and continual personal growth.

Throughout this book, we have explored various aspects of living with ADHD, from understanding the condition to managing it effectively in different stages of life. Here is a brief summary of the main points covered in each chapter:

Understanding ADHD: We delved into the definition of ADHD, its symptoms, and how it manifests differently in women compared to men.

Navigating childhood and adolescence: We discussed the challenges faced by children and teenagers with

ADHD, as well as strategies for parents and educators to support them.

Into the workforce – thriving professionally: We explored career choices, workplace strategies, and professional growth opportunities for individuals with ADHD.

Personal Connections – Relationships and Social Life: We examined the impact of ADHD on personal relationships and provided tips for improving communication and building stronger connections.

Motherhood and ADHD: We addressed the unique challenges faced by mothers with ADHD and offered strategies for managing daily routines and parenting duties.

The Golden Years – ADHD After Menopause: We discussed the impact of ADHD on retirement planning and provided tips for managing finances and preparing for the future.

Actionable Takeaways

Establish routines: Create daily routines and stick to them as much as possible to manage time and stay organized.

Seek support: Build a support network of friends, family, and professionals who understand ADHD and can offer guidance and encouragement.

Practice self-care: Prioritize self-care activities, such as exercise, mindfulness, and adequate sleep to improve overall well-being.

Set realistic goals: Break down tasks into smaller, manageable steps and celebrate achievements along the way to maintain motivation.

Advocate for yourself: Be proactive in seeking accommodations and support at work or school and educate others about ADHD to reduce stigma and misconceptions.

Empowerment and Acceptance

It's important for individuals with ADHD to recognize and embrace their unique strengths. While living with ADHD may present challenges, it also offers opportunities for creativity, innovation, and resilience. By accepting ADHD as part of their identity and harnessing their superpowers, individuals can cultivate a sense of empowerment and fulfilment in their lives.

As we conclude this journey, I encourage readers to continue their engagement with the ADHD community and prioritize their personal growth. Here are some actionable steps to take:

Join Support Groups: Seek out online or local support groups for individuals with ADHD to connect with others who share similar experiences and challenges.

Stay informed: Stay up to date on the latest research, resources, and treatment options for ADHD through reputable sources and organizations.

Advocate for change: Advocate for policies and initiatives that promote ADHD awareness, education, and access to resources in your community and beyond.

Celebrate progress: Take time to celebrate your achievements and milestones, no matter how small, and acknowledge the progress you have made on your journey with ADHD.

In conclusion, living with ADHD may present unique challenges, but it also offers opportunities for growth, resilience, and self-discovery. By embracing your superpowers, seeking support, and taking proactive steps to manage ADHD effectively, you can lead a fulfilling and meaningful life. Remember, you are not alone, and together, we can create a world that is more understanding and supportive of individuals with ADHD.

THANK YOU

Just wanted to let you know how much you mean to me.

Without your help and attention, I couldn't keep making helpful publications like this one.

Once again, I appreciate you reading this book. I absolutely enjoyed writing it, and I hope you did too.

Before you leave, I need you to do me a favor.

Please consider posting a book review for this one on the platform.

Reviews will be used to help my writing.

Your feedback is extremely helpful to me and will help me to generate more. upcoming books in the information genre.

I would love to hear from you.

Dori Natasha Gentlekins

References

Acc, L. M. (2022, June 14). *7 Critical Stages of Career Development for Adults with ADHD*. https://www.linkedin.com/pulse/7-critical-stages-career-development-adults-adhd-lynn/

ADHD in relationships: Finding intimacy when the world feels very different - CHADD. (2022, May 24). CHADD. https://chadd.org/attention-article/adhd-in-relationships-finding-intimacy-when-the-world-feels-very-different/

Anderson, D., PhD. (2022, December 5). *A Survival Guide for Parents with ADHD: Strategies from Preschool to High School*. ADDitude. https://www.additudemag.com/parenting-with-adhd-strategies/

Cfp, D. D. (2023, August 12). Navigating Retirement with ADHD: A Financial Planner's Guide. *dewittcm*.

Coghill, D., Banaschewski, T., Cortese, S., Asherson, P., Brandeis, D., Buitelaar, J., Daley, D., Danckaerts, M., Dittmann, R. W., Doepfner, M., Ferrin, M., Hollis, C.,

Holtmann, M., Paramala, S., Sonuga-Barke, E., Soutullo, C., Steinhausen, H., Van Der Oord, S., Wong, I. C. K., . . . Simonoff, E. (2021). The management of ADHD in children and adolescents: bringing evidence to the clinic: perspective from the European ADHD Guidelines Group (EAGG). *European Child & Adolescent Psychiatry*, *32*(8), 1337–1361. https://doi.org/10.1007/s00787-021-01871-x

Faraone, S. V., & Larsson, H. (2018). Genetics of attention deficit hyperactivity disorder. *Molecular Psychiatry*, *24*(4), 562–575.

Fullen, T., Jones, S. L., Emerson, L. M., & Adamou, M. (2020). Psychological Treatments in Adult ADHD: A Systematic review. *Journal of Psychopathology and Behavioral Assessment*, *42*(3), 500–518. https://doi.org/10.1007/s10862-020-09794-8

Jacobson, R., Hinshaw, S., PhD, Quinn, P., MD, & Nadeau, K., PhD. (2024, February 28). *How girls with ADHD are different*. Child Mind Institute. https://childmind.org/article/how-girls-with-adhd-are-different/

Josel, L. (2021, February 18). *How Can a Mom with ADHD Build Consistent Routines?* https://www.linkedin.com/pulse/how-can-mom-adhd-build-consistent-routines-leslie-josel/

Le, A. (1996). Sex differences in ADHD: Conference summary. *Journal of Abnormal Child Psychology*, *24*(5), 555–569. https://doi.org/10.1007/bf01670100

Mowlem, F. D., Agnew-Blais, J., Taylor, E., & Asherson, P. (2019). Do different factors influence whether girls versus boys meet ADHD diagnostic criteria? Sex differences among children with high ADHD symptoms. *Psychiatry*

Research, *272*, 765–773. https://doi.org/10.1016/j.psychres.2018.12.128

Other disorders and pregnancy. (n.d.). https://www.tommys.org/pregnancy-information/planning-a-pregnancy/planning-a-pregnancy-and-mental-illness/other-disorders-and-pregnancy

Personal Injury Claim & Compensation Guide for Non-lawyers - Injury Claim coach. (2023, December 12). Injury Claim Coach.

Polanczyk, G., De Lima, M. S., Horta, B. L., Biederman, J., & Rohde, L. A. (2007). The Worldwide Prevalence of ADHD: A Systematic Review and metaregression analysis. *the American Journal of Psychiatry*, *164*(6), 942–948. https://doi.org/10.1176/ajp.2007.164.6.942

PsyD, M. F. (2021a, December 13). *You are not the sum of your ADHD challenges*. ADDitude. https://www.additudemag.com/low-self-esteem-adhd-women/

PsyD, M. F. (2021b, December 13). *You are not the sum of your ADHD challenges*. ADDitude. https://www.additudemag.com/low-self-esteem-adhd-women/

Rooney, M., PhD, & Rooney, M., PhD. (2023, October 30). *ADHD in teenagers*. Child Mind Institute. https://childmind.org/article/adhd-in-teenagers/#:~:text=Teenagers%20can%20cope%20with%20ADHD,and%20handle%20potentially%20risky%20situations.

Sosnoski, K., PhD. (2021, September 14). *Coping with Heightened Emotions When You Have ADHD*. Psych Central. https://psychcentral.com/adhd/coping-with-heightened-emotions-when-you-have-adhd#when-to-seek-help

Sreenivas, S. (2023, May 15). *ADHD in Women*. WebMD.

UNTC. (n.d.). https://treaties.un.org/Pages/ViewDetails.aspx?src=TREATY&mtdsg_no=iv-15&chapter=4&clang=_en

Wymbs, B. T., Canu, W. H., Sacchetti, G. M., & Ranson, L. (2021). Adult ADHD and romantic relationships: What we know and what we can do to help. *Journal of Marital and Family Therapy*, *47*(3), 664–681. https://doi.org/10.1111/jmft.12475

Yellin, S., Esq. (2023, July 20). *Your rights to ADHD accommodations at work*. ADDitude.

Lange, K. W., Reichl, S., Lange, K. M., Tucha, L., & Tucha, O. (2010). The history of attention deficit hyperactivity disorder. *Attention Deficit and Hyperactivity Disorders*, *2*(4), 241–255. https://doi.org/10.1007/s12402-010-0045-8

Printed by Libri Plureos GmbH in Hamburg,
Germany